Jo Jo in Outer Sp

Jo Jo in Outer Space
© 1999 Creative Teaching Press, Inc.
Written by Margaret Allen, Ph.D.
Illustrated by Jennifer Beck Harris
Project Director: Luella Connelly
Editor: Joel Kupperstein
Art Director: Tom Cochrane

Published in the United States of America by:
Creative Teaching Press, Inc.
P.O. Box 6017
Cypress, CA 90630-0017

CTP 2923

A little orange ship flew in outer space.
The little green man in the ship sat very still.

What made that scary noise?
The little green man moved slowly to the back of his ship.

"Yikes! Who are you?" asked the little green man.

"I'm Jo Jo. I wanted to go into outer space, so I hid in your ship on Pine Cone Cove. Please do not be angry."

5

"Did you save my ship after it sank in the cove?"

"Yes!" said Jo Jo.
"I saw your ship sink in Pine Cone Cove."

"Slowly, I pulled it out of the cove.
I saved your ship for you. Then I hid in it.
Please do not be angry."

"No, I am not angry, Jo Jo," said the little green man.
"You saved my ship. Do you want to sit up front with me?"

"Oh, yes!" said Jo Jo.

Jo Jo and the little green man looked down. "Look, little green man!" said Jo Jo. "Home! Wow! I like outer space!"

"So do I, now that you are with me, Jo Jo.
Now I can talk to you. Now I'm happy."

"Yes," said the little green man. "I like that . . . pal!"

Then the little orange ship zoomed deeper into space with the little green man and his new pal, Jo Jo.

BOOK 23: Jo Jo in Outer Space

Focus Skills: simple word endings: -er, -ed, -ly, -y

Focus-Skill Words		Sight Words	Story Words
aft**er**	sav**ed**	talk	front
deep**er**	want**ed**	want	please
out**er**	zoom**ed**		
ask**ed**	slow**ly**		
look**ed**	angr**y**		
mov**ed**	scar**y**		
pull**ed**	ver**y**		

Focus-Skill Words contain a new skill or sound introduced in this book.

Sight Words are among the most common words encountered in the English language (appearing in this book for the first time in the series).

Story Words appear for the first time in this book and are included to add flavor and interest to the story. They may or may not be decodable.

Interactive Reading Idea

Have your young reader reread the book to find words that contain the root words *deep, out, ask, look, move, pull, save, want,* and *zoom.* Do this one word at a time. Show your child how to frame the root word by covering the ending (*-er, -ed, -ly, -y*) with a finger, and then how to move it to reveal the whole word. Tell your young reader that learning this new reading tip will help him or her "blast off" to good reading!